Due to the nature of this book, rea
to protect the identities off all invo
are those of my own perception a

Surviving Childhood

My name's Sylvia. I was only three when he died.

He died three weeks before my fourth birthday. I'm not sure if I understood what had happened or if any of the others did, I don't remember. There was six of us; I had two brothers and three sisters. The order went Jay, Martin, Emma, Gracie, me, and then Kim. Kim was months old and already she had to say goodbye to her dad. I was told that we preferred our dad to our mum and to be honest it's not something that I find hard to imagine. To this day each one of us misses him but then we think back and remember what kind of person he was, an abusive man with a nasty drug habit. He was something for sure; he wasn't a saint but tell me something... who is? We were young, far too young to experience the feeling of loss. It still happened.

My dad died of a heart attack on the 3rd of December 2004.

And here comes the big question that people are almost too scared to ask, what caused it? News flash, what didn't cause it was the real question we had to ask ourselves. There were lots of reasons, smoking, drugs, family history of heart trouble, and of course, stress. The worst part for me is that even the small details about him, I have forgotten - what he looked like, how he spoke, what his favorite things were and how he dressed. It was never his name on the school forms, it was never him that had to provide for the family, and it was never him that laid down the rules and told us right from wrong.

Even though it's been over ten years, we still are haunted by his memories. It's hard knowing someone with the same name as him, I have trouble saying it. It hurts when my mum talks about him, knowing how he really was completely ruins the idol I've made up and imagined in my head. She talked about him as if the darkness had completely intoxicated him and he was incapable of seeing the light. For her, he was a monster who couldn't be saved.

When things got particularly bad Mum would tell us we were going on an adventure. We would pack only the essentials and flee for safety to the nearest women's refuge. I tell myself that Dad's intentions weren't to put us in harm's way or intentionally split up our family, but the reality is I'll never be able to justify how he acted towards her. Surprise, surprise, My Mum would always go back to him, after the numerous letters and pleading phone calls.

He used to write letters to us, as I was a baby there wasn't much, he could say to me. But he still wrote a string of "go go ga ga's". In one letter he spoke about how much he missed me and how he had bought me a bracelet for the next time I saw him. I was obviously unaware that the next time I saw him I wouldn't be able to keep him for long.

Without my dad's presence, it was all down to my Mum.

She tried her hardest, but it never stretched far enough and like most single parents, she needed help.

I guess you could say my Mum was the light before all the violence, or so you can only hope. But the darkness soon smothered her too. It snapped her, inside out, until she was clinging on for dear life in hope someone, anyone, would save her.

The only person she saw willing to help was dear uncle. They say, "We accept the love we think we deserve", she was desperate and took his help disguising his evil for something else. She found herself falling deeply in love with this man; everything about him drew her in. To her he was flawless, he promised her a life of security and happiness. To everyone else he was the devil, his aura like a bad smell. She got so caught up in his world that the good was blinded to her and her job of being a responsible and caring parent was ruined. Everything she did, she did it for him.

We were forgotten, left behind.

There are so many details, and not enough time to explain, my Mum, my uncle and us kids had a massive journey ahead of us and I will probably at some point tell you what happened to them. But this is my story, I would have been the happiest child alive to tell you how everything turned out good in the end.

Life doesn't work like that though does it?

Faint memories

Faint but clear as day at the same time. My memories of being young are pretty much non-existent, up until we stayed with my uncle. I remember the family atmosphere. We were a big bunch; there was always people in every room. The school routine, my favorite dolls, friends - they are fuzzy. It's a common thing that if you've experienced traumatic things at any age then your mind blocks it out, and it is very hard to regain these memories.

I wasn't that lucky because I remember him. Dear uncle, I was so young, and how you frightened me.

You were a short man with scaly, white, skin. You had fingernails that always seemed to be dirty. You were going bald with old age. That good gene of fine, thick, dark hair that ran in the family was coming to an end. You dressed like an old-fashioned farmer, with tweed hats and jackets. Worst of all you smoked; you smelt grubby and dirty and it lingered everywhere throughout the house.

Almost suffocating.

You would call your family meetings in the living room at least once a week, all five of us kids squeezed onto the one couch. It was like a detention center; as soon as we sat down we were stuck there, trapped like your prisoners in the place we were meant to call home. You sat in your special chair that no one else could sit in, and throughout, when your temper breached breaking point, you would stick your chin out and grind your awful crooked and rotted, teeth together. Meanwhile, the youngest, Kim, played on the floor without a care in the world. My mum would be hovering somewhere near. She never felt near, always distant.

She never helped us.

You would roar at us for stupid reasons. You were in charge, and the boys often rebelled because they were teenagers and they did not like you. You did not like *this*. Us girls were stupid, naive, immature. We were only children. Every time you asked one of us a question, of course, we were too frozen to answer. But you wouldn't wait for a response before you went off on how we were "dummies." That's what you called us. We lived and breathed that word, that's all we meant to you.

I remember physically holding my breath, because I was so worried you'd hear the little puffs of air, going in and out of my lungs. My legs would cramp from sitting so long in such a small spot and at those points of time, I physically would have done anything to leap into my mum's arms. But she was as scared of you as all of us were. She did nothing but stare hopelessly through us, soulless. She knew all too well what you were capable of, and the demons you were fighting within your mind.

One day I remember having to sit for so long, squeezed onto that couch that I almost became part of it. I needed the toilet badly that day, but you wouldn't let us move, not for any reason. I didn't even need to ask you because I knew your reply would have been an instant no. The tears threatened to fall but I knew you would take this as a sign of weakness, and I couldn't face seeing your smug and gloating smile hover over me at my suffering.

I shit myself on the couch that day.

I think it's time to start having the conversation about you and what you did to us.

The older ones got it much worse than I ever did, but even so, their pain was all around me. I remember all of us kids going on day trips in the fields behind our house, the older ones built a treehouse there and to us, it was our safe place. We went to hide from you here. No matter how cold or how rainy it was, it was the only place that felt warm because you were the coldest being I had ever met and to be near you, was to be permanently frozen, lifeless.

I hated you, with every bone in my body. I had never hated anyone before, but you were different My mum loved you. This to me this was something that I found very difficult to comprehend. It always felt like she was under a trance. She as a person had been abused, controlled and manipulated her whole life by men, so this for her was the norm. She allowed her children to be treated this way too because she didn't know any better. But as a parent, she should have. For a seven-year-old, you were the scariest thing in the world. You were the monster under my bed. You were the bad man that came and got me when I was misbehaving.

You were the evil.

With every week that passed, I never got used to the strength of your voice and how every word would make me shake that little bit more. How your eyes felt on me, uncomfortable and foul, the fear that would boil up deep inside me and made me feel like I needed to be sick. It never got easier, not with you.

Coming and Going

They told us the day before, that we were leaving, it was 2008, we moved four days before my 8th birthday. A new life, new opportunities, and new people to fabricate our wonderful life to. Dear uncle had gotten a new job as a bus driver, so he convinced my mum how wonderful it would be to move. Being so young, I saw this as an adventure, I was so excited. The older ones weren't as optimistic, they were leaving much more than I was, they had friends, their school, they were furious. Of course, my mum shrugged them off, and replied only with "this is what is best". Almost as if she believed it herself, but those were obviously not her words.

It was such short notice that we ended up leaving so many things, this angered dear uncle, wo woro sluck in a car with him for at least six hours while he drove to our new home. The energy in the car that day was extremely tense. We arrived at our destination, the landlord went over things with the adults while we went to visit my granny. We ended up staying with her for a few weeks till they got the house sorted, I eventually started my new school when the schools went back in January, and everything settled in, it felt normal.

A benefit of moving here was that we were surrounded with family, from my mum's side, my granny, auntie and her kids. The older kids took great comfort in this, they went there as often as possible to escape from dear uncles' tight leash. My granny and auntie soon realized there was a deeper issue than us disliking dear uncle, so they investigated.

This resulted in Emma leaving.

He did horrible things to Emma and at the time my little head couldn't even imagine what it was he had done. Emma made my mum choose, dear uncle or her? My mum was consumed with the "love and care" he provided for her, so she chose wrong. This ended up with Emma, an innocent 14-year-old being shoved into care, which is a lonely path to be forced into, for any child.

After this happened, I knew for sure dear uncle was my enemy, I had no proof other than his sickening personality, but this confirmed everything I thought about him. I didn't understand what had happened to Emma at this age, but as the years went on I worked it out. From this point onwards, she came back and forth, and we started having a lot of social work contact. There were also times when uncle wasn't allowed to live with us, for our own safety. This was strange to know people cared for such a thing as safety. He went to stay at B&B's for months at a time, and mum would go visit, for she couldn't deny her lover anything he asked of her.

Us three youngest girls, didn't really take much notice of all this, people coming and going had happened so much that it become a norm. Jay wasn't really in the picture much, he forever took mum's side, so therefore this meant dear uncle's side. He was loyal and didn't get involved in family drama. It did however have a massive pressure on Martin, he had to look after us while mum went out to visit *him*. In return she would buy him drink, that was their deal. He was troubled and would party almost every night to escape from reality.

For the last time Emma came back, we were having dinner in the living room, they were chatting about dear uncle and how much they didn't like him, in front of my mum and us young ones. We were still blind to what he had done to Emma, she was trying to make us see. My mum flipped, she told them both to leave and they laughed not taking her serious. Then just like that everything changed. She packed their bags as they screeched at one and other, I was oblivious to the fact I wasn't going to see them for ages. With all the commotion, I barely remember it.

Emma went back into care for good and Martin went to stay with my granny, who thankfully lived in the same town. I never saw him though, ever. A piece of this house was missing, but I was made to believe that they had chosen to go. My mum told me so many stories to manipulate the events, until I was completely loyal to her and wanted nothing to do with them, especially Martin. So, I subconsciously hated him, he sent letters and I would barely look at them, he called, and I said I was busy and couldn't talk. It came to a point when I didn't even see him as family anymore. This was down to dear uncle, even though he wasn't in the house, he had control over everything. He was slowly but surely getting rid of us one by one.

Visiting Hours

Social work had a very large involvement in my teenage years growing up, either it was weekly visits to check up on how our lives were going, or big child protection meetings, and every so often visiting hours with dear uncle. I was made to believe by my mum that he was good, but I never really understood why we had to have social workers with us to see him at the time if that was true. It was for our own safety though, they sugar coated every second of those meetings, to "benefit" us. We always went to this old building, not far from our house, Gracie, Kim and myself as we were the only children left living with my mum. Seeing him in this light, made him seem dangerous, and almost criminal, those ladies with their badges were the only thing standing between him and our innocence.

That was frightening to think.

We sat with juice and biscuits while we spoke politely to someone who seemed like a stranger now. He looked as though he had been rough sleeping it, his once short and tame beard was now shaggy and overgrown. He was scary to look at some days, his face sagged with the regret and guilt that weighed him down like boulders on a dead body. I used to think that this was a normal occurrence and every family probably had someone like him. Someone that they had to keep secret from people from fear of being judged, but I was naive, and this of course was not the case.

I had to lie a lot to people when I was younger, mostly my friends, "What did you do last night Sylvia?"
"Oh nothing, had a catchup with half the social work department and my pedo uncle, just your usual Thursday

night" ... it wasn't something I could just say to people. There were rules, these weren't spoken about, but they were expected from me to keep the peace within our crumbling family.

The weird thing is that he wrote us letters when he couldn't stay with us, mostly filled with pointless things like, "you better be helping your mum out and doing your homework". Although under completely different circumstance, looking back at this situation reminded me of the ones my dad sent when he couldn't stay with us. Funny that, the two brothers having the same consequences and neither of them learning from their mistakes. I guess that's how my family works, continuous mistakes and no one wanting to own up or take the blame for it. We plead, manipulate and bully until we get things back to "normal" or how we want it.

A Different Side

It was so confusing when Emma left for good. I never knew where she was staying, if she was okay and if she was safe. It scared me so much knowing that things could change so fast. Hardly anyone talked about her, just like dad. Except she was still alive, and I was certain she was a good person. Everyone told me that I was too young to understand anything and of course, like any child, I was very frustrated at this. Why wouldn't they tell me? I missed her so much.

All I wanted to hear was her cheery laugh one more time so that I knew she was alright. Things went from bad to worse, I guess for everyone. Kim, the baby started thinking my uncle was the best thing in this word and she sometimes even called him Dad. That itself broke my heart. It was tough not knowing my dad, but it hurt so much to see that she didn't even know he had existed.

Ever since Emma left for good I started seeing uncle's 'true colours'. Everywhere I went I could feel his presence, my skin crawled thinking about 'him'. His eyes followed us everywhere; his Old Spice scent was everywhere. He wouldn't leave. Even when he was out, we could feel him near us, suffocating me from life and any possible happiness. To this day it makes me sick thinking about him. He was everywhere; it felt so dark, lonely and cruel. It's kind of felt as if he were haunting all of us. He knew all our fears, all our past and he scared the shit out of everyone. It soon became clear what he really wanted out of looking after us.

Now, when I say I started to see uncle's true colours, what I really mean is the more twisted side to him. When people ask what it is dear uncle had done to me it's difficult to find an answer.

Mentally he destroyed me, like he destroyed everyone, they called it grooming.

The things he would say to me were so wrong, and I knew they were wrong but it's not like I could have stopped him saying those things. The only thing I could do was try to avoid those dodgy topics he seemed to love to discuss. I tried my hardest to blend into the background; I kept myself to myself and tried to speak to him as little as possible.

There would always be days when I'd slip up and he'd catch me off guard, and I'd have to talk to him. That's the thing about life, we must adapt to survive, and understandably I just wanted to live. One summer, I had come back from the shops with my mum and was trying on new shorts. Which I was very nervous to wear because of wandering eyes but it was one the warmest summers I'd ever experienced. Anyway, he had crept up the stairs and stood sneakily behind my bedroom door, watching my every move. Barely clothed I turned around and saw him in the corner of my eye. Screaming "Get out!" He chuckled. I found the closest piece of clothing and shielded myself with it.

I grew angrier with every second that passed as he stood silently and watched me with a grim smirk. "Can I help?!" I yelled, trying to keep my voice steady. I started to shake; fear clutching at my heart. "Where did you get those legs from?" he questioned, admiring them intently. "Muuuuuum!" I screeched. He flinched back, almost physically hurt that I didn't want to join in with his deluded games. As he scurried away scared he was going to get caught, I leaped to my door and slammed it shut. Falling to my knees I burst into tears, relief flooded through me as I realized I was somewhat safe from him.

It could have been much worse, and I had to thank the universe every day that passed where I was safe and away from his grasp. I stuffed my new shorts to the very back of my cupboard, promising myself I would never show a piece of my flesh again if he was alive. I was unaware at the time, but I wasn't the only one who feared him like that... Gracie was feeling the exact same, although a million times worse because she had been captured. Her innocence was already gone, and the real sort of suffering had begun. The battle she was facing was much worse than mine, but my time was coming, I could feel it and so could she. It was almost as if dear uncle was preparing me.

Not long after that awful encounter I was in the main living room reading one of my favorite books. Normally when uncle would come into a room I'd instantly walk out and find myself a hiding place in the mansion we called home. But this one occasion he walked in and seated himself directly across from me. As I began to rise out of my seat he grunted and said "Sit down" with a menacing tone. I straightaway had to obey this order. I carried on with my book being sure not to make a single ounce of eye contact with him. The room filled with a deafening silence and I could feel my heartbeat going at an irregular pace. He started strumming my dad's old guitar, tuning it so it could be played. Out of nowhere he decided to spark up some conversation. "So, I haven't played your violin yet." The room went quiet as I forced myself to be nice.

"Yeah, it's upstairs, do you want me to go get it?" I smiled sweetly and waited for his reply. He burst out laughing "Nooo, not that violin." I began to get very confused, if he didn't mean my violin with its four strings and long wooden bow made with horsehair then what did he mean? "What do you mean?" I asked, wanting answers.

"You know what I mean" I shook my head furiously "Sylvia stop being stupid, you know what I mean, don't you?" his face screwed up as he thought of another way to describe it. But he didn't need to, by the look on his face I knew straight away. When it finally dawned on me I broke out into a horrible blush, the truth settling in. I felt like hysterically crying, running into the safety and comfort of my mum's arms and trying to convince her to get rid of this shallow and mentally unstable person cho called her lover. I was so scared, what was going to happen?

I sat for ten very long minutes, trying to pluck the courage to run out the room and flee for safety. I was too late though; Uncle stood up from his seat and began slowly walking towards me. He reached out his wrinkled and dirty hands to grab me. I shook violently and leaned back, wishing that the cushions of the couch would open like the doors of Narnia and welcome me into the world of fairytales and happily ever after. I squeezed my eyes shut, forcing out his horrible face from my mind, trying to wake myself from the nightmare that had sprung onto me during broad daylight. Her timing was perfect, her timing was everything. Mum launched herself into the room at first looking happy but then looking furious. "What's going on here?"

Clueless

Of course, after some sweet talking and a string of lies that mostly consisted of bitter manipulation, mum turned to me. She held a strange look in her eyes, one that was very much displeased; I knew he had twisted it. I sat and told her word for word what had happened. But she still held that look, still doubted her own flesh and blood over the man that came so close to bringing great harm to me. He had told her that I was naïve, young, and that everything I said was to make her turn on him. Emma tried to do the same thing, I was her double, out to get him in trouble and to split up this family. Although Gracie had told me snippets of things he had said to her too so why was there even a hesitation of doubt that what we said might be true?

From that moment onwards, I subconsciously started to hate him even more, and everything I did was to spite him. He created such harsh and bitter atmospheres in our daily lives, so I tried to make him feel like we did. It worked most days, but sometimes it took up so much energy being nasty to him that I had to give myself a break. He always caught me out when this time came around, he misunderstood it as me warming to him or suddenly liking him.

One day Gracie and Kim had gone out with my mum to the shops. They were getting baking ingredients as it was the holidays and we needed something to occupy us for a while. I stayed behind as I had already started a shortbread mixture. I had learnt how to do it in school, so it was a one-man job as I didn't have a recipe ready for anyone else to help. I measured out the ingredients from memory, so they were a bit off. The mixture was too sticky, and it was too hard for me to stir. So, I shouted dear uncle through, he waltzed in with a book in one hand and his glasses in the other. "Can you help me with this please?" I asked uncomfortably. He nodded away as I gave him instructions, soon enough it was in the oven cooking away.

I took a seat to rest before I faced the massive pile of dishes that were stacked messily bedside the sink. Uncle copied me but then turned to me and just stared. He did this a lot, stared randomly at me, sometimes I had an uneasy feeling he was checking me out. I always called him up for it though, and it annoyed him so much, he hated being confronted, so people rarely did it. I stared blankly straight back at him.

"What?" I said.

"Sylvia, do you know that you're really special?"

"What's that meant to mean?" I screwed up my face in disgust, was he calling me special like how they nicely describe the disabled?

He chuckled, and I awaited his answer... "Not that kind of special, just listen. This will be our little secret, okay? I think you're really special" as soon as those words rolled of his lips I knew straight away what he meant. I had heard that saying before in films, that what they would always say to the victims before something bad would happen. He was like them, those evil men. Everything now made sense, every single detail clicked into place. He didn't care about us, only what he could do us.

A frightening feeling spread through my stomach as I processed what he said. He grabbed the salt and pepper and set them out in front of me. "Now, this salt represents you, white and pure. The pepper as odd as it seems represents me. We go together, and one can't be without the other, at the end of the day opposites attract... Although people prefer the salt to the pepper, so the pepper is sometimes left on its own. But then there's the ketchup" he leaned across the table to grab the ketchup and I edged backwards, as I tried to force him out my head. "Now the ketchup sometimes interferes and gets in the way. And it sometimes it's good with salt and pepper but sometimes it can be too much...can you guess who the ketchup is?" I slowly shook my head, barely moving an inch.

"The ketchup is your mum. So, we need to stick together, okay? Because we don't want her getting mixed up in what we have here. So, what do you think about that Sylvia?"

Priorities

I of course was never one for keeping secrets, especially secrets that involved dear uncle. So, like any other normal person, I told my mum. The next day flew by and I could hardly hold it in any longer. Gracie, my mum and I gathered round the table, tension clung in the air as I swallowed loudly. "Mum I need to tell you something, about uncle…He was being really weird and saying stuff" I shifted in my seat uncomfortably, bowing my head unable to make eye contact.

"What?" my mum said in an annoyed tone, I looked up, her face resembled sheer panic, but her eyes said otherwise. They had a glint in them, as if she already knew. How could it be I thought to myself, surely, she wouldn't stand for that! Gracie started twitching, fidgeting with her sleeve, she wouldn't look at me. What's going on?

"He said he wanted it to be our secret…he was creeping me out. Mum I felt really uncomfortable" I explained. That's when she started laughing, did she not believe me?

"Sylvia that's the way he is, he was probably just joking around…he's a lot older than you so you probably took it the wrong way." Tears rushed to my eyes, why would she say that?

"I wouldn't say it if I thought it was okay" I retaliated, raising my voice. Gracie met my eye, looking concerned.

"Mum he said stuff to me too, why can't you kick him out?" Gracie piped up, looking hopeful.

"What! How can you say that? He's done so much for us, he practically raised you. You girls don't know what uncomfortable means!" said mum defensively.

"Yeah but mum he's a weirdo, what if he like says something else? What if you're not there? No one even likes him." I nodded vigorously in agreement with Gracie, she was right. Mum sighed in reply, aggressively slamming a cup on the granite counter. Meanwhile the boiling kettle almost mirrored her body, steam practically coming out her ears.

"I'll sort it" mum snapped, unconvincingly. Tears spilled out of Gracie's eyes, I took a minute to properly look at her. She hadn't seemed the same lately. I had noticed marks on her arms? And she always wore hoodies and joggers, why was she hiding herself? She looked ill, dry skin, chapped lips, wild and knotted hair. I shot her a small smile; she stared through me, rejecting it.
I wanted to ask if she was okay, but she had her barriers up, she was always so enclosed and defensive. I didn't want to upset her more, but she worried me. "Want to play the Sims? Half an hour turns each?" She giggled, while smudging her tears into her hoodie sleeve. "It's my turn first!" and with that she ran off to the play room, it took me a second to register what was happening but sure enough I ran straight after her. We landed in a heap on the floor, laughing like a pair of idiots.

She truly was my best friend, there was only around a year and 10 months age gap between us, but sometimes I told people we were twins. We were inseparable; it was like we had the same minds. She got me, and I got her, we had a bond like I've never seen before. I told her everything and she told me everything, or at least that's what I thought at the time. But as time went on, we grew apart; life changed us and made us complete opposites. Don't get me wrong, we'll always be sisters, but I'm afraid we are no longer twins.

Something came between us, I suppose uncle came between us...

He ruined her and made her something she wasn't, he made her a victim. He made her into someone who hid in the shadows, someone who feared the unknown and change. He ruined my Gracie, and I'm not sure I'll ever get her back.

The Whole Truth and Nothing but the Truth

What goes around comes back around, right? We finally had the courage to tell the police what happened, how uncle started saying things to me and how he had been sexually abusing Gracie. It was one of the hardest things I've had to ever do. Emma, and I met up at school for some lunch, she was still in care, so I never got to see her. We were catching up and having a laugh when she suddenly went quiet. We went for a stroll round the school and she told me about how recently dear uncle had been talking to her again and saying weird things.

She confronted me and asked if he'd said anything to me. I played stupid and said, "Nah not really, I don't know." She started talking about a book, uncle had shown her a passage in this book about an older man liking a younger girl and how he knew it was wrong, but he believed it was alright to have an age difference in a relationship. When she told me I started crying, "He showed me that book too Emma." It felt so unbelievably good to finally tell someone.

She took my hand and rushed me to the school's guidance department, somewhere she had become very close with. The guidance counselors demanded to know why we were both so upset. Emma stalled and told them that if we decided it was for the best then we would tell them, but in the meantime, we needed a quiet place to talk to sort a few things out. They agreed and showed us to a room, checking up on us every so often.

We dipped in and out of silence; trying to come up with a solution to the mess we seemed to find ourselves in. It went on for hours, plotting and conniving our grand plan. We had numerous conversations about Gracie, and if we should involve her. We got the guidance team to call her out of her class; looking very wary she entered the room and shut the door. "What is it? What's going on?" she questioned.

We told her it was best if she sat down, when she found a comfy position she faced us for answers. Emma went through the recent events that had taken place; Gracie said uncle had mentioned the book to her too. We all decided to call mother dearest, to see if she could help us, as we didn't want to straightaway dive in too fast without properly thinking things through. Emma pleaded with mum on the phone for a while, she gave her an ultimatum for her to kick uncle out the house and out our lives full stop otherwise we'd have to speak up about what dear uncle was really like. She refused repeatedly and said that we had to finish our school day and she could handle things. We put our trust in her, oblivious to the fact we had heard that line many times before and she had done nothing. Emma started crying, nothing hurt more to see her upset, the strongest person I knew, crumbling next to me like burning paper turning into ash. She made mum promise to fix things and make our home safe again. Mum hesitated at first but soon enough agreed.

Gracie and I went home that night, feeling relieved, hopefully mum lived up to her promises and he was gone by now. We were anxious to what awaited us after we walked through that front door. We were confused to find everything as normal, but much to our surprise dear uncle was still here. The devil had her wrapped around his dirty, fingers. He had manipulated her, one of his best skills. And convinced her into thinking we were being childish and had imagined this "inappropriate behavior" we had told mum about. She turned on us when we needed her the most, lied to us at our weakest point. If this was the parent, we were blessed with then we were destined to live a poor and wicked life. We all sat in the main living room, she sat by while dear uncle screamed and balled at us, at how we had no idea what the word inappropriate meant. How we were nothing but stupid, pathetic little girls. He said that we had no idea how hurt he was that we would think he could be like that. He demanded apologies, he demanded our pain, and so he earned our fear. Words can't even describe how that day felt, a million emotions flying high; it was as if we weren't allowed to hang onto any of them for too long. I did nothing but lie awake that night, petrified for the future that had yet to come.

When the next day arrived, I had no greater wish than to see him gone. So, like the day before, us three Cairney sisters met and decided we would tell the police of uncle's monstrosities. We swore to each other we would tell them every single detail. Emma had already tried to get justice for the evil that was brought upon her, so she was very aware we needed every ounce of information, so the police could gather enough evidence, for uncle to finally pay.

Before we had our statements taken, me and Gracie were talking and thinking about what life was going to be like after we got rid of the monster that was supposed to family. Gracie rose from her seat, interrupting our conversation and told me she had to go do something. For some reason a horrible feeling begun to erupt in my stomach, the kind where the air starts to feel clammy and your stomach feels like a million moths are trying to escape.

The next thing I'm going to tell you is probably one of the most horrible things I've ever felt or seen. Emma and Gracie came into the room; Emma tried to avoid my gaze "Sylvia we need to tell you something." As soon as she said that I knew something was wrong. They didn't even need to say anything, as soon as I looked into Gracie's eyes I broke inside. I saw right into the windows of her damaged and defeated soul. The glint they had, revealed a world of darkness and even though she tried to hide it with a blunt look, her eyes revealed it all. Those colourless eyes that day revealed a lot. Something that had been hoping and wishing for not to be true. We were too late; uncle had already got her. I had no words, but to be honest she didn't expect any.

It was time for my statement, I remember it like it so vividly, my palms were sweating, and I could feel my heart beating so fast, almost like horses' hooves on an old dirty path. Every so often I would pause and wonder if I was doing the right thing. I started crying at one point...I was so nervous I wanted nothing more for him to be gone. Everything I said to the police that day I doubted as soon as it rolled off my tongue...I had been conditioned to think this behavior was okay for so long that I struggled to pick out the good from the bad. We stayed at the school till almost eight that night. I was so relieved when I had my statement taken. It felt so unreal, he would be punished, and he would suffer, like he made everyone else suffer.

I read one day that running is the most exciting part after you've committed a crime. So, once he had figured out that the police knew about what he had done he went on the run, the police were searching for him. This was the most frightening part for me I think, not knowing where he was or if we were in danger. I remember going to stay at my grannies so that if dear uncle came back to our family home, then we wouldn't be at risk of anything. It was so strange to see him in this light, because it wasn't just us girls that seen him as unsafe anymore, the whole world seen him for who he was too. That was a reassuring yet unfamiliar feeling for me.

It was a couple of days later that we learned he went to the shop and bought some rope. He went to a forest a little while away from where we stayed, where people went walking everyday with their pets and families and instead of facing everything, he tied a noose round his neck and took the easy escape. Then some poor person had to face finding his limp body hanging from his chosen tree.

They'll have to live with that memory forever, and if I ever meet them I'll apologize a million times over. Such a selfish act caused so much chaos, a helicopter was sent out to look for him, because he was a wanted missing person, and it sadly crashed. You might have heard about it? It landed on a local pub in Glasgow and went up in flames? Killing quite a few people? That's on him; I despise him even more, for still destroying people's lives even after he killed himself. Even though it's one of the most brutal ways of suicide, he didn't deserve that opportunity.

He had hung himself.

I wanted him gone, but not like that.

Teardrops

I remember being told that he had died.

All of us gathered in Mums living room, sorrow draped across the room like ugly, charity shop, curtains. My mum made it sound so tragic. Kim started howling, her legs got weak and she collapsed on my mum. Her cries were deafening. The rest of us sat in silence. It hurt, not that he was dead, but that he didn't have to pay for what he did.

I looked around the room. My mum and sister huddled together, grieving. Emma's eyes went glossy and she looked down. My brothers were trying to keep control, comforting everyone. Gracie shot up for her seat and yelled "It's my fault, it's all my fault!" Jay leaped to her side, gripped her arm and pulled her into a tight hug. He whispered soft, comforting words in her ear. He looked at me, eyes full of sadness.

I sat still, frozen. All colour drained from my already white face and I felt absolutely nothing! No emotion came. Martin looked at me, and I looked away awkwardly. I wasn't sure where to look. Everything was a mess. I didn't know what to do. Don't get me wrong, Dear Uncle was alright sometimes. Everyone has good, people just hide it more than others. I had known this man for as long as I could remember and suddenly, he was gone.

About a week later, it was time to say goodbye, for real this time. It was the first time in a long time that my whole family was together. The funeral was here. Not many people showed, my uncle's brother and sisters, me and my family. I could hear soft whimpers from my uncle's family sitting behind me. Everything was quiet, almost peaceful.

The room was only half filled, but that didn't surprise me. Uncle was a bold character, you either liked him a lot, or hated him, there wasn't really an in between. Pretty flowers and fancy bibles were everywhere; I couldn't help but think, did he really deserve this kind of sendoff? Everyone pretending they cared for him? His brothers and sisters in the row behind me hadn't contacted him in almost four, maybe five years? Surely that was saying something?

The worst part was when my uncle's body was getting taken out of the room. That's when a tiny part of me realized I would miss this old man, his kind side. I made a dramatic sigh; they had started playing our song. 'On the road again'. It had been a joke me and dear uncle had, when he wasn't being an absolute creep of course. He was a bus driver, and when he wasn't working he was always taking us places in the car, so I would always sing that song to make fun of the fact that was all he ever did. When I heard those four words I let it go, tears streamed down my pale cheeks. My hands shook. Emma pulled me to her side and rubbed by back in a comforting way.

It was time for us to leave. My mum snatched me from my seat and literally dragged me out the room. It was too much for her. My face, now soaked with tears, buried in my mother's side…my tears staining her blouse, mingling with the tears shed from her own eyes.

I felt drained.

He was gone.

The emotions in the room was so overwhelming, I think that's why I cried, not for him, for all the pain bouncing off everyone. Or at least that's what I've been telling myself.

Unforgettable Battle Scars

Gracie's self-harm had gotten serious. When I looked at her, I wanted to wrap her up in a hug and heal her, regardless of my own pain or even abilities to do so. My mum and Gracie didn't have a relationship at all, they never talked anymore. I always find this kind of ironic, how could my mum be whispering with her in corners or amongst chaotic family meals one second and then almost instantly have nothing to do with one and other what felt like a second later. They were always on the same team, yes both, with completely different intentions but the focus was dear uncle. Rip him from the equation and it all falls apart. Mum felt guilty that she couldn't protect her children because she was blinded by jealousy at the fact uncle showed us more affection than he did her. But Gracie didn't want regrets, she wanted answers and most of all justice that sadly she would never receive. Why her? Why *our* family? Her cuts got deeper and deeper and no matter what people told her she wouldn't stop. She couldn't see that by inflicting pain on herself she was inflicting pain on us too.

I tried it a couple times myself. The pain was horrible, but it felt good in a way. It overpowered the pain deep inside. I knew it wasn't right, but it was like an escape. My arm was my canvas and the sharp blade was my paintbrush. I stopped after a couple of times. It was a relief to get my emotions out, and when things got extremely bad to handle, it always tempted my mind. But seeing Gracie, in the state she was and the effect it had on her health was so worrying, I couldn't watch her slowly kill herself and then do the same thing.

Although for Gracie it wasn't so easy to stop. At first, I pitied her. Such a pretty girl and such ugly scars. But it annoyed me more and more as I saw cut after cut. Fresh or old, it made my skin crawl. Why would she want to hurt herself more, hadn't she been through enough? I was scared for her, what would happen if I lost her? Whenever it came up in conversation she would always tell me that she did it for us, the only way she could live with us was to harm herself. That was heartbreaking.

For me freedom was enough for me to begin healing, but she was stuck in a box with all that pain, and no matter how hard she tried to push the lid off, it stayed shut. Almost as if dear uncle was sitting on top, holding her down.

Trapped.

I told Gracie about the life she could have, with happiness and freedom, but my words could not bring her out the box either, no matter how many attempts. Much to my defeat Gracie would show a small smile, not really taking in what I was saying but accepting I was trying to help. She was a very stubborn person, in the sense that once she had something in her head, she was the only person that could change her own mind. I found it difficult to be around her when she was like this. She was sad, and no matter how many jokes I would throw at her, or how many stupid things I would do to see her smile, none of them worked. She turned her music on, turned it up full blast and sung to her heart's content.

Singing was one of her coping mechanisms; she could do it for hours on end, song after song, and would never get tired of it. So, I would sing with her, both of us taking it in turns to do a line or two. Her voice was obviously better than mine, but if I could help her, even if it was just a bit of company doing a simple thing like singing then I didn't care what I sounded like. Although we did get a few complaints from the neighbor's mind.

Behind Closed Doors

I came to realize after dear uncle died that I saw most of the male race in a different way. I was self-conscious and worried about what people would think of me, especially men. I felt like because one man had such a negative impact on our lives, that all men would be the same. I found it extremely difficult to trust anyone as I assumed the worst of people. I started to see men as no more than predators towards children, especially in school, where children were vulnerable to figures with authority. I started to assume that every relationship and marriage were full of anger, violence, and sexual abuse.

It wasn't always like this, we were happy once.

We would do fun things. Dear uncle liked taking us places, little adventures he said. We'd go to the shops and hang out a lot together. We'd go to lots of famous landmarks. Going long walks and looking at ghostly castles made us seem normal, like a proper family. There were lots of skeletons in our cupboard after all. We were normally surrounded by crowds of tourists or innocent bystanders; we had to act as if we hadn't a care in the world. Even when we were all in the house, we sometimes did fun things. We would rent a movie for the night or play board games. Uncle would always think of jokes and sayings he thought were funny. We laughed even though most of the time it wasn't anywhere near funny. He would always buy us treats, like chocolate bars, or sugary sweets.

He was nice sometimes, he was thoughtful. He would always listen to you when it was your turn to talk. He would consider that sometimes you could be upset or moody. He would try his hardest to make you smile, even if he wasn't happy himself. It was almost if he had a personality disorder, or he was bipolar. He always changed the way he acted; how could we relax...never knowing which side of uncle we were talking to? One minute he would be a genuinely nice guy and then the next thing you know his evil eyes would be on you and he would say something inappropriate. An evil person is like a dirty window, they will never allow light to properly shine through.

Even though I speak about how evil he was, the reality is he was ill. Pedophilia is a common mental disorder; it affects the brain in different ways. Most people think that people are just born to think these things; they act differently towards people for pure pleasure. It makes you say and do certain things you wouldn't normally do. It makes you think that hurting people sexually and emotionally is right. I'm not saying what they do is okay but there is a logical explanation for everything, I must believe that. I only hope that now he's gone we can get on with our lives and live up to our full potential.

I never really thought about it much when uncle was alive, but he had a lot of strange habits and pet hates. He was a very short man and hated it when anyone, and I mean literally anyone commented on his height, people avoided bringing it up with him. Or if he saw someone of a different skin colour he would call them a name and discriminate against them. But if you said anything about them, even if you were complimenting their shoes, he would go crazy and call you a racist any chance he could get. He was the biggest hypocrite I knew; it was the exact same with people of different sexualities. He was very old fashioned in the sense that he thought the bible was the only rule book;

anything different or unique was bad. Which in this day in age was a ridiculous way to think and could have gotten him in a lot of trouble if he had been caught saying anything of the above.

I thought that after everything died down with dear uncle, we would surely be able to move on, live our life with our new friend; Freedom. But as you may already know my family isn't that lucky. I myself was trying to deal with the aftermath of it all. Figure out who I was, what I wanted to be. My mother still acted as if he were alive. All his cruel rules and suffocating terms were still in place. Once again, she was left to be a single parent. He thought it was only right to bring us up the way he had been brought up, one shower a week and one change of clothes for a week. While other kids were convincing their parents to buy them their first phone or a new pair of jeans, I was convincing my mum, day and night to be allowed to wear two outfits a week instead of one. It was so embarrassing, and I felt so ashamed when I saw my friends more than once a week after school and I was wearing the same pair of clothes I was wearing four days ago…and they had a fresh set on. I always sneaked the odd shower, when uncle was away out shopping, or my mum was occupied with Kim or Gracie. There was also the case of, the food on the table was the food you ate, and no snacks were allowed in-between meals. The heating shouldn't ever be on, it costed too much, if you were cold put a jumper on. No talking back, ever. During the day you were to go outside and play, even if it was raining, you'd live. And yes, you may think these are all very petty things to be complaining about…but were you shoved outside as soon as it turned daylight with nothing, but a breakfast bar shoved in your hand and told not to come back until dinner time? Did they lock the door on you and leave you to starve outside all day no matter what the weather was?

It was very much so the case that if Kim wanted something you gave it to her, and if she asked you to play you never got to say no. It was always the same, when he died these rules were in place. Of course, I rebelled as much as I could over the years, going for showers more often, turning the heating on 'by accident' and sneaking into the kitchen and stealing half its contents. I think back to before his death, two and a half years ago we would have been sitting, frightened. Frozen in one spot as soon as he entered the room. Scared to get changed or shower in case he was there, watching. Scared to open your mouth to speak, in case it was the wrong thing to say. Even scared to swallow in case it was too loud.

He would straightaway stick his chin out and grind his awful teeth together. Then his nostrils would flare, and his eyes would look as if they were going to pop out of his sockets. He would wait for you to finish speaking; giving him time to think of what bitter words he could spit out at you. Suddenly you would not only hear it, you would feel it. His monstrous voice would be unleashed, and you would literally flinch back frightened. His devious little body would walk right up to you and he would poke his chubby fingers in your face. Without a doubt he would be standing there for a good hour ranting and raving, picking out all your flaws, and mistakes.

To think that I used to fear this man, this disgusting little weasel. If I was ever confronted by him today I would have no trouble having it out with him. Stand up for myself like I never did. Prove that he was the one in the wrong. Make him feel like he was worthless and stupid. I forever dream of doing this but then I realize that he isn't even worth my time. I always wonder if dad was still alive would all of this of happened. Would've he have protected us against monsters like dear uncle or was he one of them? Would he have done the same to us? Abused us like he did mum? These are all questions that will never be answered but I'm glad, because some secrets are best left untold.

Dear uncle's close relatives told us a short time after he died that he was a rapist and a violent man. His sisters told us horrible stories of when they were younger. Their mum and dad died when they were all young and as Uncle was one of the oldest, he watched over everyone. These things I'm about to tell you, I have difficulty even believing myself. Dear uncle whipped his brothers' countless times with chains off motorbikes, He beat them up till they wore black and blue. He raped and sexually abused his sisters for many years. This person was meant to be someone they could look up to. I can't go into too much detail because it's not my story to tell, but you can only imagine how awful it would've been. Words can't even explain the pain and heartache they must have gone through. They would have all been young and unaware that these things were wrong. It was so long ago that these crimes were not spoken about in that day in age. But then we also must consider the fact that these people then went on to have children and allowed dear uncle to breathe the same air as them…why would you risk it?

Do You Believe in Angels?

People say there are such things as angels, I guess you can say it's a myth but I myself think we all have an angel that watches over us and guides us through our journey called life. Over time I guess the people we think are our angels change as we see life clearer and for me my angel was Meredith. She appeared one day at my mum's side. Literally glowing with love and happiness, she had silver and almost angelic hair, with a smile that could make anyone feel at home. She said to my mum that she had been sent to her to help her guide her onto the right path, Dad and dear uncle had sent her.

They had told Meredith that they were reunited when Uncle passed over into the afterlife. They said that when you die you are forgiven for your sins and mistakes. Mum was overwhelmed to hear this stranger talking about her two ex-lovers almost as if they were still alive. I know she didn't have massive white feathery wings or a golden halo but to me she was an angel, inside and out. By now you will probably think I'm going insane or conjuring up a person with my imagination. I can happily tell you that Meredith was very much real, and she just happened to be a medium, so she was very much in touch with her spiritual side. Mum and Meredith straight away became good friends after that, they held onto each other for support and shared their deepest darkest secrets with each other. That was until Emma walked back into mum's life and met Meredith. They straightaway clicked and step by step Meredith began to heal Emma's broken and damaged heart.

She began gluing all the shredded pieces of her heart together that dear uncle and Mum both helped to destroy in the first place. Ever since Emma lost Mum and Dad she had been searching high and low to find someone to fill in their role, someone she could be fully attached to, with no chance that they would suddenly turn on her or leave. Emma finally found she could rely on, someone she could love, and someone that would love her. Meredith was naturally good with people; she was a great listener and excellent at giving advice. If it weren't for her I probably would have been put in care again. She acted like mum's mother most of the time, practically giving her parenting lessons. Things were always good when she was there; she had a way of controlling any bad situation. I guess with every person in your life that you treasure, there comes a time when they move on and that time for Meredith came too quickly for me.

She went to live with Emma and they started to build a life with each other were there wasn't any chance of family destruction. They left me with the monster I called my mother. I was alone and the feeling of being depressed still hadn't passed. Her frail and weak body screamed at me for help as she smothered me with wicked blackmail and something that she thought was love but in fact was as bittersweet as her. One night it got too much, I threatened I would run away and tell anyone I went near how horrible she was. Tears streaming down my frightened face I sneaked to the back door where I unlocked it and quietly scurried out the garden and into the very much unknown, dimly lit darkness. As I started to pick up my pace into a run, sparks of adrenaline streamed through me, the good feeling of freedom came to me and the sad tears soon turned into cheerful ones. I ran as fast as I could to my real family, my siblings. Meredith had now earned the title of my sibling, she was the older, wiser sister that I never had, and she was still my angel, from a distance. So, they shielded me with their love and attention, and took me to a safe place that I now call home.

A Weekend to Remember

I was sucked out of deep thought as the grumbling of the car came to a halt. My trustworthy social worker Holly, a crazy lady who was always chuckling about something or other, looked at me cautiously: "Are you ready?" she said. This was a different side to her that I didn't get to see often. She was normally a bold, witty character who said what she wanted, when she wanted. She always looked out for my best interests and took everything I said on board, so I trusted she knew what she was doing when she picked this family. I nodded shyly, unsure I was after all doing the right thing. I didn't have to be here, there were other options:

Residential? Distant family? Two things I was as anxious about as this new home.

We climbed out of the car and made our way to my new home. The house looked tiny from outside, almost as if the front of it had fallen in; giving the impression it was smaller than it was. The dark, wooden, front door was all I had left shielding me from the unknown life I was about to experience. Hands trembling, I reached for the metallic buzzer. There was a short pause and then a clatter of footsteps. The door handle started to turn, and my stomach erupted into a tornado of butterflies. It was time to meet my "new family". I was welcomed in by a cheery, middle-aged woman called Gabriele. She had dark, bushy hair that bunched up messily on her broad shoulders. She was a plump lady with soft, kind eyes. She beamed at me and ushered us into her spacious living room.

I sat there quietly, an overpowering and controlling voice inside my clouded head screeched at me to sprint out of the house and abandon the whole thing. Holly introduced me as Sylvia. Gabriele and Holly went over paperwork and chatted for a bit, while I zoned in and out of their conversation. "Sylvia is a very, very, nice girl; you'll learn to love her, honestly she's great." I laughed to myself. Did she really think that?

I looked around and took in my new home; it was more than spacious. I got a sense that everything oozed organically. Dark and light browns all combined, with a massive bookshelf and a long stretched out window revealing an acre of golden, fruit trees and freshly cut grass.

I felt relieved finally to be here, but still wary of meeting the rest of the family and settling in. It was time for Holly to leave; this made me emotional, I was so afraid of being left behind the anxiety of it all was eating me up. We had had so many arguments and misunderstandings over the years I'd known her, but she was the only thing familiar I had left and that frightened me. We had come a long way together and I felt like she was abandoning me.

"Well I better be on my way," Holly glanced at me and I gave her a small smile, masking the pleading face I was pulling in my head for her not to leave me. She stood up and brushed off her uncoordinated and random clothes which always left me hoping she'd have had an extravagant makeover the next time I saw her. She would always wear this shaggy and out of date purple jacket, with a fluffy collar that had seen better days, with random green polka-dot print tops, grey cotton cords, which in my opinion looked awful. She would tie the whole thing together with some strange looking pumps that always had a colourful flower attached to the sides, and of course she had five pairs of these shoes all in different colours. If anything, she made me chuckle upon seeing her, and her unchanged dress sense.

"Right have a good time Sylvia; message me if there's any problems, okay?" I nodded even though I didn't have any credit left on my phone. We said our last goodbyes. I heard a click from a distance: Holly had left, and there was complete silence. Gabriele hurried back to the living room. "Would you like to see your room?" I raised my eyebrows when she said my room… "Yeah, that would be great" I murmured, uncertain of myself.

I followed Gabriele like a lost puppy. I felt so completely and uncontrollably lost. My emotions were flying high all over the place, the reasons I had to come here and why I had nowhere else to stay we're getting to me a lot. I could feel tears starting to form, my lips beginning to tremble. I sprinted upstairs to my room in a hurry to hide myself behind a closed door; something I was more than used to doing. A million tears spilled out of my worn and tired eyes. I felt the lowest I had ever felt in my whole life, not even when my dad died, or when I was taken off my mum had I felt this low. There was so much I didn't have that I wanted that everything else was blurred and unimportant.

I had unforgettable memories of my mum's clingy body which screamed out to me for unconditional love and attention. She forced her role onto me, demanding I give her motherly care as if she was the child. Digging in her bony and unintentionally sharp claws she would rip all strength and willpower out of me, draining every ounce of energy from me to make herself feel stronger. You might laugh when I say this, but she is the kind of mum you only hear about on the news with headlines like "Daughter Starves

While Mother Parties" or "Mother gets Away with Child Neglect". Looking back, she'd always been the same, putting herself first, acting completely and utterly selfishly and thinking she was still a teenager without any responsibilities. As a child I was oblivious to what she was like but as I grew older she became a lot clearer.

I craved the feeling of being loved, the warmth of family, and the care of a mother. I broke down onto the bed provided for me, something that didn't even feel right calling mine. As usual no one came to my rescue, not even my so-called new family, they didn't even check on me to see If I was okay, or even still alive. I cried myself to sleep, finding comfort in the fact I was practically unconscious.

Sleep was the only safe place I had left.

I woke up the next morning to find a wild looking, black, cat peering at me from the end of my bed…where had it come from? Thinking back, I did remember Gabriele mentioning she had pets but how did it get here? I giggled quietly as it stretched out on top of me. Feeling somewhat better I mirrored its actions, completely forgetting what day it was and cozied myself into my blankets.

There was a knock at the bedroom door. "Come in." I said. Someone peeked their head round the side of the door; it was Jack, Gabriele husband. I had met him last night: a nice, cheery man. He gave me the vibe that he was a people pleaser, always looking out for others. He was tall, with a scruffy beard and eyes that practically popped out of their sockets. His old, tired face looked at me in surprise: "Oh, I thought you would already be up? You better hurry, you'll be late for school." He said it in calm tone, not at all worried I had less than 20 minutes to get ready. He shut the door and left me in a chaotic mess.

Running around in all directions I tried to retrieve my misplaced pieces of clothing. Realizing I left my uniform at my old home; in such a rush when I left; I forgot to take it with me. I had a flashback of the look on my mum's face when Holly told her I couldn't live with her anymore. For one millisecond it crumbled into a million pieces, and then suddenly, she said "that's fine" putting on a menacing frown. I sighed as reality came back to me and I heard Jack shouting for me to hurry up.

I gave up and chucked the first thing I saw on. Practically falling down the stars I tried to hold on to any dignity I had left and went and got some breakfast Gabriele offered to take me to school as I would need to get a bus pass for the future. This overwhelmed me, I felt forced to settle in here, forced to live here forever.

The car journey was pleasant; honestly, the conversation was just reaching the mark of pleasant. Gabriele said the usual "How'd you sleep...the weather's good today...argh traffic's terrible." I mostly stared out of the window, taking in the beautiful, morning sky and the seas of green fields. When we arrived at the school, I said a short goodbye and then abandoned the car.

As soon as it was out of sight I rushed into the school, tears streaming down my face. I got disapproving looks from the people in uniform, judging my choice in clothing. I passed a couple of classmates, who gave me concerned looks but no one asked what was wrong. I didn't even knock on the guidance office door, just walked straight in and planted myself on a chair at the children's support workers desk. I sat for a while, trying to get my words together. I hated talking about my feelings, it made me feel weak. They gave me worried glances, and told me not to bottle it up, something I did often. They asked what they could do to help and then I broke. I pleaded with them not to let me go back. I wanted to go home, to my real home. No matter how bad the situation had gotten with my mum, I was willing to deal with it. I couldn't face staying with a house full of strangers any longer.

I felt so out of place and had no idea what to expect. Each day seemed to pass so slowly, which made me feel even worse as I was overthinking about my mum, my new family, the feeling of loss, and how scared I felt, plus I was getting upset every five minutes. I had never thought what foster care would be like, like thought about it in good detail. I wasn't prepared for how surreal and strange it felt.

Like, have you ever been at a new friend's house and you feel a bit awkward asking for juice and something to eat, like you almost feel a bit rude asking? That is literally most of your day in one sentence. You don't know what your boundaries are or your limits. Don't get me wrong the people I stayed with were lovely, very caring and sweet, but that sort of made me feel even worse about asking for stuff, or even talking in general, in case I said something wrong.

I will never forget the experience though; it has made a massive impact on my life and changed me for the better. It was all a blur, but it was a big thing for me, to stay at my placement. It had known other people in care, but then suddenly it was me in that position and not them. It changed me for the better because it taught me to be more patient, I stayed there for a weekend, if I had stayed there a couple more nights I might have liked it, and I might be getting on better than I am right now.

It also taught me not to put all care kids into a category. When anyone I knew would talk about their experience I would stop them mid conversation or zone out. All I thought they were doing was attention seeking or being drama queens. Looking back, I fully regret being so judgmental because I hadn't experienced what they had been through or could even have imagined what it felt like for them.

Parents

The constant screeching, she would do, claiming we were a nuisance, the countless times she would drink her sorrows away to numb herself from the pain she felt inside, and all the times she would lock us outside for hours on end so that she could get a bit of 'peace and quiet'. It had always mounted up, until recently when I realized that I did a better job raising myself than she ever could.

While we were going cold and our bones were starting to show she was hiding from the frightful monster we called our dad. Every day she would acquire new marks, almost as if someone had clarted dots of black and blue paint all over her weak and tired carcass. She was stuck in an inevitable cycle of abuse; it surrounded her everywhere she went, which meant it surrounded us too. When I was younger my mum was my ultimate idol, and I ask myself why all the time...what if I didn't know wrong from right because of watching her and became the type person she was, how would I end up?

All the memories I have of her she was always sobbing in the background or floating around the house like a ghost, too scared to move, or say anything. I wish she had been stronger, and stood up for herself, stood up for us. She had never been there for us, how many times as a child did you have a cold and wanted your mum? How many times has your mum chucked you a sandwich and told you that's all you're getting for the day? How many times has your mum been blinded by her own pain so much that she could never give you affection and the care you needed? These are the things I know too well; the things that I've grown used to, tell me how would you feel?

My mum had a lot of demons, I can't really say it was bad for me because that was all I had ever known. She let me down so much as a child. If she had been more focused and in the right state of mind things would have been so different. Not having a mother or a parental figure for most of my life impacted me massively, but it taught me to be independent from a really young age, and to take the good with the bad. And that just because people make inhumane choices, doesn't mean they're evil people. It's also taught me that I want to be nothing like the role model my mum has made herself out to be, each day I grow and learn I know that whatever choices she would have made, I'll be making the exact opposite.

I always felt sympathetic towards mum, always thought she tried her very hardest after everything she had been through. I always wonder how she lost sight of what was happening with Gracie and dear uncle. Mum's dad, (our granddad) had sexually abused her for over 12 years. She knew the horrors of abuse and isolation, how could she let it happen to someone else? All I can say to that is all children deserve parents but not all parents deserve children.

She let her own children live with this monster…the children she carried for a long nine months and gave birth to. There have been rumors that she knew what he was like before we moved in with him. It disgusts me how history has repeated itself; my entire family is filled with abuse, hatred and heartache. Why have they all failed to protect themselves and their children?

For a long time, I felt I had to protect mum, look after her, and stay loyal to her. This proved difficult as it should have been the other way around. I now see that she walks around as if the world owes her something. I had many arguments and fallouts with her about how she acted or her lack of emotional understanding about dear uncle. I stayed at my grannies on and off when things got bad, until one day I ended up in a foster placement. I think that hit my mum hard, I was her second youngest baby. I was there for four days; it was such a strange family. They were probably the closest thing to normal you could get. It was strange to me because they were a real family, with nice rules and sweet conversations.

Now I find myself staying with Martin, my brother. It's calm and peaceful at his house. I finally feel like a child, like someone's looking after me. He takes his time to listen and help me through any difficulties I have. He provides for me like a normal parent would. He cares; he cares a lot, it's a strange feeling to be loved. It takes time to become a child again…if you ever can!

It's always difficult when new friends or teachers ask about your parents. I always go into panic mode, I remember when I was in primary school and I told people that my dad worked in a different country, so I never got to see him. I was too scared to tell people that he had died when I was little; I guess I didn't want them to be friends with me out of pity. The same thing happens when someone starts talking about how strict or annoying their mum or dad is, they go right round the group until they come to you and you are speechless. You tell them that you don't speak to your mum and they straight away want to know why. To them it's unnatural to not speak to their parent's everyday so they are curious.

After you clean up the mess about your mum they ask about your dad and as soon as you mention he died or he's no longer with us, their faces drop. They straight away go resort to apologies and their eyes fill with sympathy. It generally tends to be an awkward conversation killer. My mother's a very stubborn person; she doesn't "understand" why I don't stay with her.

That hurts, to know that she won't even try and figure out why another one of her children didn't want to stay with her. The worst part is she acts as if she knows it all and that the world revolves around her. All that matters is that she's okay, that she's not worrying if she's going to have to suddenly abandon everyone and go into a foster placement the next time things get bad. Or if one day people will give up on her and she'll be all alone. But I guess that's another part of life, some people don't understand certain things, and they don't get that the good people should be held onto and treasured. Not forgotten about or chucked away when not needed.

Drowning

Drowning in icy cold water, the kind of water that grows arms and legs and screams at you with thirst. A thirst that will eventually be satisfied.

Life can feel like it is dragging you underneath the surface, forcing you to believe that these last few gulfs of air, aren't yours to keep. Maybe, just maybe, you don't deserve the privilege to breathe Earths air. Why, you wonder? I'm getting to that. The fear of not managing to pull yourself above the surface that's intertwining you with death himself is something I find myself forced to face daily. You see part of me maybe doesn't have the courage to fight these rogue waves that are out to get me. So, while I'm trying to pull myself above the water, I know deep down I'm not really giving it my all. Realistically if I sink to the bottom, it wouldn't be a loss. The water craves me and my darkness. Giving in to it would end all suffering.

You see whenever uncle did anything to the other girls it was mostly at night, there was numerous occasions when I would wake up and he would be sitting on the end of my bed just watching me. He always said that he would get to me one day and it was even more worth it because he had waited so long, and now that he was dead, I would never know if he did get to me or not. The thought always lingered in my mind, I was a very deep sleeper, would I have even noticed? The unknown and the unanswered was the scariest thing in the world after he died.

I can't help but go over everything from my past on repeat, over, and over, and over. I dwell in a world of my own to the point of having a "bad day", or at least that's what they call it.

And of course, there is no special elixir to this awful thing called a bad day, no magic wand and no magical potion. Today was one of those days, but ten times worse. My vision kept getting blurry, cold tears leaked out of my bloodshot eyes, crystallizing instantly as they fell to the ground. All I felt was an overpowering ache. I could feel my shoulders get heavy and my breathing, ragged. Dark thoughts consumed my already damaged mind.

A shiver crawled up my back, bringing me back to reality, making me get goose bumps. It was the changing of the season; winter was almost here. I was sitting by the river, on a pretty little bench, with a tall tree next to me. A vast amount of leaves were dancing in the wind, everything looked so wild. I loved seeing all the colours change and the leaves glide ever so elegantly through the chilly breeze. I was lost in my thoughts, going over and over everything. I was so tired; I didn't want to be here anymore. What was my purpose? I breathed in the fresh clean air. I was thinking of all the things I would miss. The beauty of the world, my family, my friends. I wanted nothing more to jump in the river and float away. Sink and let my spirit run free. I wanted it to be over. I didn't want any more "bad times" or "hurtful disasters".

I started seeing a darker side to the shadows and shady parts of any room or place I went to, they seemed so much more sinister and gloomier. I wanted to die but couldn't kill myself. At the same time, I wanted to kill my emotions and feel okay again. I felt as if I was locked-up inside my own body and there was no escape.

I found it extremely difficult to speak to anyone about how I was feeling. As soon as I came near to speaking about it to someone the words would somehow disintegrate from my mind and the water works would start. It was torture keeping all these emotions in, I had all these feelings all at once and I didn't know how to control them. So, I kept them locked away in a box deep inside my head, in hope that someone would find a key and unlock the secrets to finally let me be free. My mind kept wandering back to my family. How they would feel? I know I would be heartbroken if they left. Would it be the same for them? How would they cope considering the recent events?

Martin

Martin you truly were something of a knight in shining armor, our guardian angel, our brother, our role model and most of all, our friend. You were always there to save us from the evil, to protect us and keep us safe at night.

You were the good I craved so badly for our family.

When things got tough, you became that treehouse we ran to. You were our safe place, and no amount of words could ever thank you enough for being the bravest and strongest person I knew. You took me in when our mum gave up on me, and it truly was a blessing in disguise. Like any brother, you annoyed the hell out of me, and encouraged me to do things I didn't want to do, but you always had my best intentions at heart. I quite literally turned your steady and peaceful life upside down as I screamed and threw many tantrums about how unfair the world was. But you were always there to rationalize my thoughts and explain that some things in this world were unchangeable but always livable if you had the right people around you.

I think in some ways you needed me just as much as I needed you back then. You regained my faith in family every time you went above and beyond to fight for my happiness, my safety and my future. You gave me, and still give me so much to be grateful for in this world of hatred and unhappiness. Even though we were practically strangers when I first moved in due to mother dearest separating us, we grew to know one and other very well. For example the fact that you cannot live your best life with unwashed dishes, or how you milk a hangover for the entire day, or how you will sit up all night playing Final Fantasy at age 24 and then complain about sleepless nights for the entire week.

I think everyone in this world deserves a Martin, because I know I'd be lost without mine.

The Three Witches

One mum, one dad, and two daughters. Let me rephrase that...one unaware mum, one pedophile "dad" and two innocent daughters. Growing up my mum had a sister called Jasmine but there was a certain barrier between them, that was Sean, their dad. He sexually abused my mum from the age of four until she was sixteen, she never mentioned it to us ever while growing up. Jasmine was more than happy to make us aware of who and what he was. He was someone I never knew growing up, sometimes I even forgot mum had a dad at all. He was spoken about in a strange way, I never questioned it when I was younger, but I now know that if I had, my questions wouldn't have been answered.

Mum was the oldest of the two, Jasmine told me that everyone in that house knew what he was up to but her mum (my granny) was in denial about it so never stopped it from happening. Jasmine was very aware of the fact he had the power to harm her, there was times when she said that she had to physically fight him or just hide from him. While you read this I'm sure you'll find that you've heard this story before, Jasmine and I were practically in the same boat, stuck in the middle of the abuse, always trying to fight for our freedom. It is a story yet again that I'm not allowed to tell as that would be crossing a line, so let's skip ahead to the part when we moved when I was seven. It was the same town that my granny lived in, we came here most summers to visit.

My mum, her sister and my granny were called the three witches because they would tell us stories of their broomsticks and magic tricks. These were off course not true, or at least I am yet to prove this. But somehow dear uncle used this to twist our views on my auntie and granny and made those fun and light-hearted witches seem evil and wicked. So, we stayed away, never getting close enough to speak or wave. It was almost forbidden, just like a fairytale storybook. But my mum was also referred to as a witch, but not necessarily a good or bad one.

Interfered

As blunt and completely morbid as it sounds it's hard knowing that you may or may not have been the outcome of rape. My dad was a very different, human being. He was a good father, as far as I remember, but his relationship with my mum was hardly ever good. I don't remember much of him, so I always wonder why people seem to sing his praises as if he was some sort of saint.

Whenever my mum tells stories about dad, her eyes fill with sorrow, and she always looks in pain. It was almost as if the mention of his name triggers her scarred brain with all the memories of the beatings and arguments they had. I've always been scared to ask about him after he died, I didn't understand where he went and anytime I did speak about him puddles of tears would always form in people's eyes. I'm glad I don't remember the violent thumps and the trembling voices of mum and dad's arguing. Thankfully most of the bad times from when I was younger I've somehow managed to block out, so much that I there's no longer a single trace of the memories.

I think about him a lot, miss him. My mum used to say I was incapable of missing him because I was too young to remember him. But that's not true, I miss the person he should have been, the person I wanted him to be. When I think of him, all I think is what if? And I think about what sort of relationship we could have had; did we have similar personalities?

I think the worst part is hearing stories, from Emma and Martin. Turning nostalgic, their voices go mushy and they talk about the good days, drives to school or even playing with him on the PlayStation. And the bad days too, when my mum left my dad and took them to the women's refuge, when they would hear mums' whimpers because of what he did to her, or when he would get high and they would watch clueless. I want nothing more than to take the pain away from them, I almost feel sorry that they knew him, because they got to know him, and they grieve for him every, single, day.

I'm disgusted at how my dad treated my mum, she said the only time he was kind of nice was when he was stoned. He was too spaced out to tell her off or be controlling. But then that's not how I remember him to be so, what am I meant to believe? I've always convinced myself that he was a good person, and that he had very dark demons that he had trouble facing sometimes.

The thing that weakens my view of him though is that he apparently "interfered" with Gracie and Emma. They were barely toddlers and he was their dad. Gracie said she had a memory of mum giving her thrush cream, Emma had the same memory. My mum covered it up like she did the rest and never told a soul until recently. I'm always left lost when I try to have my own mind and my own opinion of what he was like and what he was capable of.

I'll tell you this though, I'm utterly tired of my whole family being victims, of them being poor and dying off without living their lives as good people. The secrets that accidentally slip out and the stories people have in my family never ceases to completely amaze me, not in a good way of course. I guess I have to say I'm glad I've been dealt these cards though, I wouldn't be the person I am today without them. Your past only defines who you are, not who you'll come to be.

Control

Do you ever come to a part in your life where you have to stop? It almost like your mind freezes and your body screams out to you. All you can think about is how you've let yourself go and put everyone first for so long that maybe, maybe you know how to find yourself again? It's like one day you get that small glimmer of hope and you know for sure that it's going to change your future? This came to me one day; it was like my mind had finally reached out and flicked that light switch that I had been desperately looking for what felt like a very long time. Something snapped inside me, and I felt again, I no longer felt numb.

That was the day I decided to shave most of my hair off. People always asked me and still do to this day why I did it. My reply was generally "because I wanted to". The truth is it was to do with control. I had no control over my emotions for a very long time and living with mum on and off well let's say I was an emotional roller-coaster. The main reason though was because dear uncle hated it when any of us got our haircut.

One time I got a little more than a short trim and he was furious. He didn't speak to me for weeks on end; No joke, he completely blanked me for three weeks straight. And then after he had calmed down he had the cheek to say to me "Aye I suppose I can forgive you then." The first thing I did was laugh loudly in his stupid face and then walked right past him, making sure I roughly nudged his shoulder on the way.

I sometimes think about how sad it is that I can't tell people the real reason why I cut my hair off, they would need to know the full story about uncle to understand. It's a lot to take in, especially for someone looking for a simple answer.

You will never understand how many thoughts and feelings I want to cram onto one page. This story has been my healer, some people say it only makes it worse if you live the past. But in fact, you can only move on and focus on your future if you can accept your past. You must slowly move through each chapter from the beginning of your story so that you can go on and make new ones. If I've learnt anything important then it would be that don't ever let anyone control you. You are your own boss of your life. It is sometimes difficult to overcome people who think they have control of you, but you must prove them wrong. I know it's not as easy as it sounds but it's worth a try.

This has taught me so much about being human, not being controlled is such a key thing to life. Freedom is such a wonderful thing that everyone should experience, you can't live your life being dominated by manipulative or possessive people. Once you break through that cycle it gets easier, much easier. Even a simple thing like gaining control of your hair is a step in the right direction. Don't ever let them think they are in your head, you can survive this.

M&D'S

I realize that I never talk about good times; I guess I'm more able to write about pain because it's sometimes a stronger emotion? I want to let you know the good times too, to show you that people can still have happiness, with all the horribly bad stuff. Gracie, Emma, Martin, and Carlos (Martins partner) and I all were on holiday down near Glasgow for a few days, among other family members. The week hadn't been as eventful as we had hoped, so we all decided to go to M&D's, a big theme park that wasn't too far away. After a million wrong turns and a few shady maps we finally found it. Everyone was a bit cranky, the journey was stressful, and we waited in the cue for at least 10 minutes.

When we finally got our wristbands, we decided to go into the 'Amazonia' and it was amazing. Our moods had been turned around within seconds, the exotic colours and wild creatures took over us as we became totally transfixed. We spent at least half an hour in there, going around and round, we couldn't get enough. There was Poison Dart Frogs, Tarantulas, Pythons, Fruit Bats, the list goes on. Our next stop was the 'Big Wheel' I have never been so scared in my life. All five of us squeezed into a cart to find that there was nothing to hold onto, we sat clueless as the wheel started to move.

We assumed that the wheel in the middle that was attached to the pole that held the whole thing together was what we were meant to hold onto. Well let me tell you now, it was bad choice indeed. As the wheel lifted off the ground and our stomachs all bounced with butterflies, the guy running the ride grabbed ahold of our cart and spinned us…yes spinned us! The wheel we were holding onto swung round, which made us all twisted as we spun round with it, ending up with some minor casualties.

Most of us erupted with laughter, but that soon died down as we got higher and higher, until we were 35m high exactly. Each one of us gulped as we looked down at the ground. Don't get me wrong, the view was incredible, but Martin and I had a squeamish fear of heights. Emma and Carlos took in the view as they took some photos, but I could barely keep my eyes open. I started singing to myself, to calm myself down. But the rest of the cart shot me annoyed looks and told me to man up. The wheel went around a total of three times, and every time it came down to the bottom we hoped we could get off early in fear that one of us might spew.

We finally got off; finding ourselves safe and sound on the ground, we stretched as our muscles had become sore and tense for sitting so long. I was shaking like a leaf; we couldn't help but laugh at each other's silliness. The next ride was one that I'll remember forever, the 'Flying Carpet'. The cue was short, we climbed on and I warned everyone that I would scream if I was scared, as it would help me. Everyone but Emma heard me so when the ride started whooshing back and forth getting faster and faster, my heart started racing and I let rip. I honestly never screamed so much in my life, it was too fast.

Everyone chuckled at me, but soon got the hint when I didn't stop screaming. Gracie gripped my arm and the huddled her head next to me trying to calm herself down. Martin shouted at me in-between laughing, clearly embarrassed by me. Emma kept giving me worried glances, thinking I was crying she cuddled me and said I was going to be fine. Emma assured me it was stopping as it started slowing down…but it was just going backwards this time. As soon as I calmed down I started screaming again. Gracie hugged me, crushing my face into her neck, for a few moments everything went blank as I passed out. It was over, and I few girls from the back row looked at me worriedly "Excuse me, is she alright?" They questioned in their Glaswegian accent. Martin giggled and said "Yeah, she's okay."

Martin helped me up as I was still shaky. Gracie stayed put though, she shuffled over to Emma and whispered, "I can't, I peed myself" Her forehead creased into a furrow. We all burst out laughing, classic Gracie; she'd always had a weak bladder. We wandered round for a while, no one would let me on any more of the rides, but that didn't stop me. Gracie and I went on all the kiddie rides and then we all went to the arcade. The day was honestly brilliant; we were all a bit upset that Kim couldn't come with us though. To finish the day off we went to TGI Fridays and enjoyed a lovely meal before heading back to where we were staying. We have a lot of days like these, we have family days as often as we can, and we all end up with unforgettable memories that are stapled to our hearts. I'm so unbelievably lucky to have these people around me; I will treasure them for life.

The Theft

Gracie stared at me anxiously waiting for a reply "Sylvia! Are we doing this or not?" She questioned in an annoyed tone. I nodded vigorously, wanting to get this over with. I stood at the wooden, gate as she scurried round the back of the house, I heard a gleeful "Yass!" and I giggled as I imagined her fist pumping the air. Gracie came back running to tell me mum had, as usual left the back door unlocked. I smirked intently "Okay we've got to be quick."

A stranger walked past the brick wall around mum's houses. We stepped back into the shadows, hoping we would go unseen; He jogged past in a hurry, more concentrated on his scruffy looking German Shepherd who looked rather excited about some falling leaf's. By the looks of things this was going to be an easy trip home.

We both slid round the back, Gracie went first. I heard a satisfying click of the door and then we were in! We crept in the kitchen and turned the light on. "Gracie stop sneaking round, people are bound to notice if we're walking around all dodgy," I advised, feeling a bit paranoid.

"Okay, okay," She relaxed her shoulders and took a deep breath, "Right you do down here, and I'll do upstairs, got it?" She commanded. She swallowed loudly and stared at the stairs distantly for a very long two minutes. I took her reaction as her being a bit frightened, in case someone was upstairs. "Go on then, you'll be fine." I smiled kindly, giving her an encouraging nod. I wandered into the living room; it felt so strange to be back. Everything was exactly the way it was when I left almost seven month ago to stay with Martin.

I messed around, trying to find anything that was Dads. Mum point blank refused to give any of us kids his stuff, she claimed that we were either too young to even remember him or that he left all his stuff to her so why should we have any of it? This made no sense at all because she apparently hated him. I was on the hunt for his guitar; it was one of his prettiest possessions. There was a silk finish over the black exterior, with a little bird at the end of the strings. He used to play it all the time when we were tiny; he would teach himself songs and then sing to us all. It was the best, or so I've been told, I don't remember that part of him. Although when I look at his guitar, or hold it in my arms, I can only think of the fact that he did they very thing once upon a time, that at one point his DNA was all over this, fingerprints and all. I feel so much closer to him when I'm with his things, they help me remember him.

I couldn't seem to find it, so I moved onto the next thing on my list:
- Guitar
- Cam recorder
- Evidence

Anything else of any importance

Now I know exactly where that would be…Gracie interrupts my thoughts "Sylvia come here!" I rush upstairs thinking she's found something… "I can't find anything, maybe look through those drawers and I'll look over here?" clearly hinting at the third thing on our list. I gave her a disappointed frown; maybe this will be harder than I thought.

You're probably wondering what we would need evidence for. You see when uncle died that was it, case closed. There was no suspect anymore, which meant the evidence was no use to them. But Gracie wanted justice, so instead of finding stuff to incriminate dear uncle, we were finding stuff to incriminate Mother dearest. Gracie was 100% certain that mum knew about Gracie's abuse while it was happening, so she was doing everything in her power to pin the blame on mum.

So, I carefully rummaged through her drawers seeing old address books I recognized, and homemade Christmas cards that we had made for her over the years. Gracie stopped what she was doing and marched around the bed "Sylvia! She's going to know someone's been in here, be more careful!" She bleated in a whiny tone. I looked down at the drawer; it was a wee bit messy but nothing that couldn't be fixed within a matter of seconds.

I hope it was clear by now that Gracie loves to exaggerate, she was always such a drama queen. "Look there's nothing here," I explained "but I do know where the cam recorder is though". We travelled downstairs and I went into the cupboard in the hallway. "Oh yes, found it," I hummed. I had to pull a few old boxes off it, but we succeeded in finding at least one thing on our list, so for that I was proud. Gracie claimed it as hers by snatching it out of my hands "Aww decent man, I'm going to watch this straight away," she exclaimed. She had always been so fond of the cam recorder, mum put all the videos on tapes and she loved watching them. There were a bunch of random videos of birthday parties, days out and normal daily life with all us six kids getting up to mischief. Gracie remembered more of dad than I did, and it broke her heart remembering how we used to be. We were one, big, happy family with only a few bad qualities and a few sad secrets.

The tapes meant a lot to her because she often found herself forgetting what it was like to be a family, and how it was when we were all together. I think that hurt her a lot, more than people realized, there were so many things she wished she could forget, but there were so many more that she wished she could remember forever. Gracie turned to be with a genuine smile, probably feeling very accomplished, "Right, we better go," I nodded in reply.

My heart felt as if it was oozing with adrenaline; I could do anything I wanted. We ran out the house, and then out the gate, I told Gracie not to lose anything because I wanted to watch some too. She gave me a distant look as a worker from her care home pulled up in the car...it was time for her to go. I wished in my head that they wouldn't ask her about what she had, and if they did they would let her keep it, at least for a wee shot. We both headed in separate directions, acting as if nothing even happened. I looked back one last time and Gracie flashed me a knowing smirk and gave me a quick wink.

Triggers

Memories have a way of latching themselves onto things, whether that's a place, a town or even one of your favorite pieces of clothing, it happens all the time. Sometimes this is good, but then sometimes this is very, very bad. The one that always catches me out is places; it makes me think of him. There's this strange sadness that's plunged upon me whenever I visit a place the whole family used to go or somewhere we would pass by for the shopping. It's hard not to get upset or lash out, especially when all there is to speak to is a bunch of strangers. You want to scream at them "This place reminds me of HIM!"

Being in a place that he used to love, makes me only think of him. I came to this place for a good reason, full of good intentions and to new beginnings. It wasn't only until I got there that I realized that I had been here before…and who I'd been here with. Within a matter of seconds my weekend was ruined, and I tried so hard to hide this from all the people I came here with. They knew something was up; either that or they thought I was extremely rude and shy.

I can hardly expect the people I'm here with to know why I'm a little bit quieter than the rest of the group or know the reason of why I can't stand to stay at the harbor or shops for too long without looking distant. They have no idea…

So many things remind me of him, or of the time of year that symbolizes loss. Anniversaries and dates mess everything up and leave me feeling in a stew. There's so much to remember, dad's anniversary of his death, Dear uncle's anniversary and the day he ran from the police, mum's birthday…that's stuck between the two like a bad omen. And then there's Christmas, the coming together of friends and families, which of course never happens in mine but still. It's going to be extra tough this year as it's the first Christmas I haven't spent with mum. The same as my birthday it will be without the woman that made my very life possible.

People keep telling me not to get upset about the time of year and to forget the dates because at the end of the day they're numbers. But it's not as easy as it sounds, I can feel the Christmas presence and all the feelings that come around this time. But I also carry all the bad memories from uncle's funeral and all the miserable stuff that I felt this time last year. It's everywhere I go and even the tiniest things trigger those awful memories and feelings.

The dull weather reminds me of the dull days when we sat imprisoned by mum and Uncle. The coldness of the air reminds me of the coldness of his heart, and when you were near him it was nothing but isolation. The powerful force of the wind reminds me of his torturous roar and his deceitful lies. I could go on for years and tell you what everything reminds me of, but I'm afraid that my friend would take forever.

I suppose I must look at the bright side though, this will be after all the first Christmas I will spend with Martin in almost six long years. That makes me want to cry and laugh at the same time, but I know he'll make it extra special for me. That's something he's very good at, making the most out of any awful situation.

Missing Them

I try not to think about how much I miss them, they are part of me, like a heart to a body. All I can do is make the most of the time we have together, petty arguments and "normal" family drama aside. Don't get me wrong I see them enough…I guess to remember them, it's human nature to want more, but in this case, I think it's justifiable. We all had to flee from the nest far too quickly; far too soon, we slipped off into the unknown. Everyone feels so distant but close at the same time.

I want to pretend we are all young again, like when I see Kim I want to grab her hand and tell her when it's safe to cross the road and carry her about the place because her little legs are too weak to walk far distances. I want to baby her but she's not six anymore, she's all grown up. It seems weird to think it's almost been a year since I left home, I always feel a blister of guilt thinking about it. Was it the right thing to do after all? I feel like I've left Kim behind, I sometimes wish I stayed for the reason of spending more time with her. I know I would if completely died inside if I stayed there any longer, and I'm not the only one.

I feel like I've already missed a lot of Kim life in the space of a year, birthdays, and special events etc. It's coming up for Christmas, two months to be exact, how am I going to do it without her? Family is the best part of Christmas, when everyone comes together, united.

I want her to see what I see, to understand what I'm trying to, and for her to lose that sickening loyalty to mother dearest. Because she'll choke every ounce of happiness out of Kim, because mum can't have what she wants and if someone else has it, then why should they be better off than her? I can't even begin to think about what goes through that woman's head. It's as hard as trying to count an infinite about of numbers. There's no end, and it's confusing, take my word for it.

It's the exact same with the others, I want it to be like the good old days when I would play games with them and have sleepovers in their rooms without the worry and dread I had to carry on my shoulders every single day. I want to relive my childhood, or at least start over and make myself a better one, so we could all be together once again.

Sometimes it feels like nothing has changed. When I think of family, it's still that mushy feeling of mixed messages. Everyone's still very hot and cold, touchy subject are still ...well touchy subjects. It almost feels like some days we linger and bury our heads in the past, thinking only negative thoughts. Some days are focused completely on what has happened, and the tiniest thing can affect your day. Especially when it comes to thinking about family, when you see a mother, father and child on the way to school, or when one of your classmates mentions how they did something nice with their sibling, you crumble, into a million pieces. Just like a paper cut, tiny and hurts a little, but you want to make a massive fuss over it.

Summertime Sadness

I came to realize some time ago I got myself in trouble with the wrong kind of people and I'm not completely sure how this happened exactly, but I regretted it a lot. Not all of it, we made good memories, but I mostly regret it because we would party and party and party again. We would laugh and sing and dance but then something happened, and it changed everything... I wasn't meant to be that girl. That girl that did stupid things I would then regret. After everything I had been through I should have known how to keep myself safe, how to keep myself from being the vulnerable one.

I had yet to learn.

I won't use names because part of me still feels guilty for what happened that night and everything since. We were both in the wrong, we should have been more sensible...soberer. I don't know if it was the alcohol or my state of mind at the time, but I was spiraling out of control. It took what happened that night to make me realize what I was doing with my life.

Ruining it.

When I was fifteen I slept with an 18-year-old. This to him was obviously something to be proud of, but I was so ashamed. He told his friends and one night my brother overheard him in the pub talking about it. They started fighting and this resulted in my brother, Martin, having a fractured jaw and the police being called. They came around and took my statement on what had happened that night. The police officers made it so much harder than it had to be, see the thing is when you get interviewed you can't assume they know what you're talking about, you have to say all the correct words or "terms". It was one of the most humiliating situations I had ever been in. All my friends fell out with me when they found out this boy was being charged with statutory rape, they were confused as to why I would accuse him of this. I of course didn't, it was just the term they used because I was underage. The called me a slut, attention seeker, and a horrible friend to this boy.

Eventually all my friends were called in for witness statements and the story came out about how everyone had taken ecstasy that night. I had a very strict rule on drugs, especially at parties where in the wrong situation, no one could truly be trusted to keep you safe, so when everyone else took their pills I pretended not to see anything and went on with the rest of my night. The older boys took control of pouring all the drinks that night, so when the officers suggested that I could have been spiked, it all sort of made sense. I would have never have normally just slept with someone, the night was so blurry and when I remember the sex, all I know is that it hurt, and I fell in and out of sleep during it and so we eventually stopped and then he dressed me in a t-shirt and his boxers. I passed out almost immediately, and when I woke he was acting as if this was a normal occurrence for him.

As the police got involved, they couldn't collect any evidence because the "incident" happened so long ago. There was zero evidence to back up the case, so he got off with it. As soon as I got this news, I was furious, he wouldn't admit to himself or others what had happened that night, and now I will never truly know myself.

Unsung Heroes

Its important to be thankful and appreciative of those who have helped you through struggles and hard times, many of them being unsung heroes to the world, unrecognized for their wisdom and kindness. I always took notice of them pair, and I wouldn't have made it to the place I am right now without their continued guidance and care. Jasmine, my children's services worker was a soul I was not worthy of, but however I was forever grateful of her presence. Whether it was hot chocolate dates, saving me from bad decisions or runaway missions, or just keeping me in a good mindset, she never let me down. And then of course, Ms. Bailey, my guidance teacher, an absolute gem to say the least. Much like Jasmine, Ms. Bailey always made time for me, even when she never had any, she always made the impossible seem possible. She wasn't just any old guidance teacher; she always went the extra mile and pushed me to be a better me in the end.

They often referred to me as fierce, a title that I was very glad to have. It made me smile, because the word fierce meant so much more than they realized. It stood for everything my mother was not and everything my sisters were unable to be. And so, it was a title I would continue on with, for as long as I could.

What I Saw

I know what you must be thinking, a girl goes through a life like that and not have a mental health issue, addiction or eating disorder, well it's true, I didn't. I experienced depression, I guess it was one of those things that was always there, lingering in the background. I also sometimes convinced myself I had body dysmorphia, but again in this situation I was lucky. My mum was always skinny growing up, and the more I learn about her the less I become surprised about this fact. His mouth was always fed first, whether it was my dad or dear uncle. And then us kids, and then her, but she never seemed interested in food. She never craved anything or found comfort in it. She was never scary to look at, I had been around this my whole life, it was normal to me.

But then it happened to Emma, and that really threw me, seeing people who are that skinny is both frightening and ugly. They look physically ill all the time; it can be unbearable to watch. This happened to her for many reasons, and then it begun in Gracie too. This is when I realized it was becoming a pattern. Since then I guess I've always had the fear I'll end up like them, fragile twigs that could snap in half at any given moment. People commented on my weight a lot, and I hated this. We had very fast metabolisms in my family so no one was particularly fat or overweight, but it meant that losing weight was very easy. This for me was not a good thing, I was constantly fighting it, it chased me everywhere I went.

I was constantly overeating to the point I'd feel sick to my stomach because I was so full, but that never ever stopped me. It used to really upset me, and I'd stay in bed all day to keep myself away from reflections and mirrors so that I didn't have to over analyze every pointy, sticking out bone I had. I guess the fear of it came from the fact that if I looked like them then I would begin to think in my head that I was them. They were all strong people at one point in their lives, but the idea of them now, frail and numb from existence made them seem weak. I didn't want to resemble someone that was weak and leached of people for strength and energy.

The fact I was skinny really limited me from going outside some days, I'd cancel plans and stay hidden because I was so scared of people's thoughts. Like depression or any other mental health issue, this fear never really went away. I come more accustomed to dealing with it each day, but it never gets easier. The front door sometimes seemed like the gateway into a different dimension, the anxiety leaving the house would eat me up that much that I'd literally just go back to bed and sleep the day away hoping tomorrow would bring me strength to live my life the way I should.

Bear Grills and David Attenborough's Love Child

I welcome the tears, the ones you force upon me. The ones you make me feel guilty for, when they spill over the edges of my clifftops for lower lash lines. They are a fraction of how you make me feel daily. So many high expectations crushed into seedlings of disappointment, constantly, over and over. This kind of pain takes toll on people, especially people like me that are told "it'll get better from here" and "you deserve the world" ...well where was it? Where was all this promised goodness, and why hadn't I found it in you?

Relationships have always been a tricky one, I guess they are for everyone. But for the people in my family the word love means something different. It is admittedly something of the unknown. I understand what it was to be loved, and to love another but the thought of it has always seemed illogical and daunting. It is bittersweet, I've never been able to grasp how someone could love another like my mum did with dad, and her dad the then dear uncle. Loving someone throughout all their mistakes and flaws, through good and the bad even when they're having mental and physical effect on your health, life and morals of what's right or wrong.

Yes, I have been loved, to an extent, by family. But not the kind that is shown or spoken, it is the kind that you were aware off, you assumed that's what it was. Although at the age of 16, I can't say that I ever let anyone that close to me, in that way. Because love hurts and love destroys, and I would never forgive myself if I ended up like her. Always loving, but never loved, used, betrayed, and broken. It's not something that I find at all inviting, but of course I am aware of the goodness of love too, and the positivity it can bring, but that kind of love seems rare to someone like me, non-existent even.

To be happy, you need to learn how to not let sadness consume and control you. It is an addiction to be sad. You get sucked in and trapped, and although I talk about the fight between light and darkness often, it isn't as simple as that. For many of you reading this you may not know what it's like to be neglected and deprived of simple human interactions. Yes, this word *is* thrown around, again a lot, but saying it, is acknowledging the fact that it happened to us. Love, like I've said previously is something in my family that always felt distant, sometimes to the point that it was questionable to even think it was real at all.

A myth.

Without attention, without love, what other good is there to feel *without* those two key elements?

I'm not shy to admit that because I have now experienced life and what it's like to live in a stable and safe household, I have come accustomed to how life should be lived. To me, the way I see myself and the life I live now is sometimes spoilt and very luxurious compared to what I had before, but that's just because I lacked the basics that every child needed to begin with. From one extreme to the other it's shown me to appreciate the little things that most people unknowingly take for granted. The point I'm trying to make is that now that I know what kind of life I should have, I struggle to cope and accept when I get given something different - this is where expectation from people comes from. Why should I get anything less than what people have promised I deserve, this kind of thinking gives me a spoilt mindset because I always expect to have it all after living without so much for so long.

Secondly, I think it's safe to say I'm a very emotional soul and things upset me very easily, and yet everyone in my family says that I'm quite closed off and don't ever speak about how I feel. To build you a better picture let's just say my "first love" was called Lawrence, although mostly referred to as "Bear Grills and David Attenborough's love child". We were two complete opposites but being with him made me realize a lot about myself; one of which things was that I was scared to be alone. Being with him and "loving him" was always the easy part, but loving life without someone to distract me from reality was difficult.

I know what your thinking, what happened to Lawrence? He had a dream of joining the army, it was something that his family believed in strongly and he wanted to peruse it. I had always told him that when the time came that he was ready, we would deal with it then, so I put it off for as long as possible. The thing is, the longer is spent getting to know this boy, the more I feared that day coming, and how his dream was going to take him away from me. I had so many people come and go in my life, I knew I wouldn't be able to face that again with someone I was so attached to.

I wanted him to stay.

Before when I lost all ties with my mum it was easier because I had so much anger towards her that there wasn't a doubt in my mind. I know we'll never have a relationship again, but she never loved me like he did so it was easy to let go. But he loved me, a much different, deeper kind of love. I had never walked away from love before, with anyone. After leaving my mum I became someone that lived her life solely based on trying to find the biggest distractions possible to hide from dealing with my pain. So, this led to drinking and being "wild" which basically just meant being stupid and getting random people to fill that hole where I was meant to feel love. He saved me from that, but I didn't know how to do it without him, or with only a distant reminder of him to help me.

So, I was at a loss, and sabotaging our relationship at all costs because he was no longer able to be with me in the way I needed. At times he was a reminder to me that love in the end never does good. It took me a very long time to let him in, for his touch to not feel wrong or for me not to be ashamed about how I felt towards a guy. He opened a part of me that I was never comfortable exploring sober, I put my whole trust in him and the promises he made to me.

But love should be better.

There was still so much that he never got to know about me. It breaks my heart thinking about how much we had been through, almost two years spent together, then for us to end up being two people that loved each other at the wrong time in our lives. I welcomed him into my life with open arms because I wanted to be loved so badly, it was the unknown. The little girl inside me wanted the fairy tale ending because I was trapped in that big tower for too long, not only trapped but tortured. My Prince Charming never came, instead he did.

Thor

Have you ever been jolted across a bus as the driver speeds off to his next destination and your left startled and embarrassed for not being quicker at finding yourself a seat? That's the kind of stomach wrenching fear you made me feel when I realized how false we had been. You worshiped me, for that short while. You made me feel like my body was addictive to you. We spent such little time together, but you were the most passionate person I had ever come across and your gaze...was truly like nothing I had ever experienced before in my life. Your eyes held something, so serious yet with grazes of light and an unspeakable need for more. You would stare into my eyes as if I held the equation of time travel or the destination of a brand-new universe.

Time stopped every time I felt those eyes on me.

I felt you, I felt you in every way possible. No one had ever looked at me as intently as you had, you had me mesmerized by your every move.

Then I stumbled across your hidden secret and believe me when I say it was the kind of back handed truth that no matter where I hid, I could not avoid it. I felt the sickest I had ever felt that day. No hangover, bad food poisoning or sickness bug could compare to the feeling. Almost as if you tore the invisible threads apart that kept my soul attached to my body. The pain in your crumbling voice that day, when you found out that I could ruin you, that's what hurt the most. Not that you had lured me in and used me, but that the Goddess from your own world was going to be heartbroken because of your infatuation over little old me.

I remember the first time I met you, and all the nerves bubbling up inside of me, you seemed like perfection...I was soon to learn that those who seem perfect truly are the ones with the worst flaws. I smiled and laughed at myself saying "if you turn out to be a murderer, I wouldn't even mind because you're beautiful". You ate this up; yup, you had me hooked. Oh Thor, I should have seen it coming but I truly was blinded by you.

For someone who looked like he had been hand made by the gods, your actions did not entertain the same qualities, after learning the truth I realized you were far from beautiful. But you see the problem is, months forward from this discovery, I find myself still truly perplexed by you. Lust is a strange entanglement, and for us, it only ever felt right. Your power this time wasn't a hammer in one hand, but instead my attention. To be enchanted by you, was the most dangerous power you could possess over me. You left to go back to your own galaxy to continue with adventures across vast oceans and hurdling clifftops, and I was stuck, bewildered by my encounter with a magic I hadn't ever imagined experiencing.

And so, I thought to myself, surely it must have been a dream. Months passed and I didn't hear or even see so much as a glimmer of you. I tried to forget your pained eyes that lingered on my skin and move on, but it was hard. You see that's the thing about magic, it's legitimacy will always be under scrutiny. I'm not even sure I wanted to hear from you again, you manipulated the powers you had, and I was the prey in your twisted game of human curiosity. But there was still something there. Whether the connection intertwining us was real for you or not, I felt every, single, earth shaking moment of it.

As if almost by fate, when everything around my world was collapsing, you appeared out of nowhere, a god sent from above. Much to my surprise, your world had also been fractured, we were two lost souls colliding by chance, everything about it seemed questionable. Your intentions were unclear, and this curdled me. But I wanted you like I hadn't wanted anything before in my life.

The magnetism between us was undeniable.

The only thing I had to ask myself was, was this genuine or purely meaningless desire?

And yes, I could use the mistake you made, and hold it against you for the rest of my existence, but people hold much deeper meaning than the knowledge we have of them in black and white. I knew you were sorry, for one of the few times in my life, when you said those words, I knew you meant it. The guilt you had for what you did weighed down on your shoulders so visibly that I almost sympathized with you.

I met with you again, almost seven months after releasing your secret to the world, and you seemed so different. This time I saw you as a person, a down to earth, normal human being without all the god like features and shining halo. You were you, and that made me feel at peace with what happened between us. Removing you from the pedestal I had you on and allowing myself to see you in this light, meant that I realized we are all constantly learning and growing. You learned from your mistake, and I learned not to be so naive and get attached to people so easily.

Home and Away Bae

An odd title don't you think? You see, people often wonder how you can feel so much for someone who is present and yet not here at the same time. But it's completely possible, and in this instance; it was very real for me. I somehow found myself being pulled towards these people that I could only have half of; all at once or not at all. When I stumbled across you; I was intrigued. You seemed different, laughable now of course, but there was something so humble about you, I saw right through your tough guy act to a little boy that needed to be loved and looked after.

You were given the title Home and Away Bae as a reference to your ruggedly handsome looks, as if you had been plucked from Summer Bay and placed before me by accident. But the name also held importance because you were in the military, and I knew I wouldn't be able to keep you forever. You see the sad part was if we had met at another time, or in different circumstances, I 100% believe that you maybe could have been the one. Unfortunately for me you weren't looking for a soulmate and a happily ever after.

I was your short-term fix.

Unlike Thor, there was so much more to us than lust and attraction, you had soul and a vulnerability to you that was so rare to come across in someone that had to literally be brave as a living. You had been hurt before, I could sense the pain because it lingered on your skin like it did mine. We could relate to one and other, and it felt nice to be more than just beautiful to someone. It was as though we just knew how to love one another, let me get this right because it can be hard to explain. We weren't in love, or anywhere near anything of the sort. But when we were with one another and I was lying with you that's the only way I can explain what it was like. We knew what one another needed and it worked. Now I know love is not something you can switch on and off, but this time around it seemed easy for us. It wasn't that we loved each other but rather the way we made each other feel, I can vouch for that at least. You had weaknesses and flaws, but there was so much more to you than perfection and to come across someone like that was so daunting.

We did normal stuff like go on dates and watch films together, but time was always very limited with us and that made me sad. I honestly had never come across someone I had so much in common with and to know it would never be anything more than casual dating hurt. I had chosen to get myself into this situation so I couldn't complain.

You were a loss that stung more than it should have. We soon called things off when I realized we both wanted different things and a different future.

I felt empty.

And as if it meant nothing to you, you moved onto another girl that same week. You see I think the problem is, I shouldn't have allowed myself to turn on and off that love switch and play with fire as easy as I had without thinking I would get burnt. There was no way it was ever going to have a happy ending, but I craved that so much, and with you, it seemed more than possible. I guess we both just needed someone at that point in our lives and we were kidding ourselves by carrying it on further.

Your absence in my life was everywhere I looked.

This kind of disappointment at us coming to an end tore me in half, far more than it did with Lawrence and Thor. I really thought we had a connection, and I'm still not sure how I managed to fabricate everything else around you to make what we had seem like love in my head.

Clark Kent

Much like the fictional character, you were someone who was very unsure of themselves, but this never stopped you from trying to help me whenever I needed you. You didn't need a badge or the superman title, because you were more than enough without it.

And so, I am forever grateful for you.

Haunted by You

I see you, not just in my dreams, but in certain qualities of other people, in objects, and in crowds. I don't think there will ever be a time where shortbread, Bacardi & Coke, or green tattoo ink wont instantly remind me of you. I don't think there will be a night where you don't visit me in my dreams and remind me of the past or how your face has been burned into my soul like a cigarette piercing into fresh skin.

Dear uncle, I wouldn't wish your existence into anyone's life.

Its funny, after almost six years, how you still frighten me, just like that monster under my bed when I was seven years old. I know after you died, I said I would have had the courage to stick up to you and I thought I'd be the one in control for once. But in my dreams, you still hold power over me, you are still the scariest thing in this world, dead *or* alive. When you visit me in my dreams, anything becomes possible, and this is not something I take lightly or with a pinch of salt. Now, I know it isn't real, but it feels real, and it brings me back to that frightened little girl I once was.

Sometimes I question if you were ever real at all, the thought of our family back then seems
like a different lifetime. Almost as if I made it up in my head, but when I see you in my dreams, I am reminded of you in every way, the fear, the uncomfortableness and the stench of your presence.

Much to my distaste, you are part of me now.

What I find most difficult, is when you worm your way into my mind when I'm with them. And by *them,* I mean all my bittersweet, childish, romances that I've previously mentioned. You always make me question if its right to have these feelings for these men. And once you're in my head, all I see is your face, the face I have long since tried to erase from my memory.

It seems funny, but I always seem to associate you with the darkness, because for long enough that's all your soul emitted. I think unconsciously, I've taught myself to be wary of the dark, and so now the fear of it is like the fear I have of you. The thing with darkness is, if you can reach the light, you must be the light, and this was something you made close to impossible for me growing up.

A Stranger Amongst Family

Much to my surprise, my mum had been getting counseling trying to work through all the trauma of her childhood. She even rekindled her relationship with her sister (my auntie). And yet, this woman still felt like the furthest thing from home, her title of a mother had lost its sentiment a long time ago, and regardless of her efforts, she would never be that to me again. And to be honest, I didn't need a mother, I didn't need to be looked after, it was too late. She wrote us a letter in hopes of explaining everything rebuilding bridges, and for the first time in my life, I read those three unknown words.

It broke me.

The wait of eighteen years to hear the words I love you, broke my heart, like an axe slicing through embers of wood. A short part of what she wrote was –

"This story is not an excuse for what happened, it's my story of trying to come to terms with my childhood and to try and make sense of why I was unable to protect you children the way I should of. I am also sorry for not showing you more, that you lot are the best thing that ever happened to me and I'm so proud of you all and I haven't told you all enough I that love you and for that am sorry.

I am always here for you all.

Love mum."

A Question of Love

It's strange to discuss love because you never really know what it is until you feel it for yourself. And even then, I believe there are levels of love, and very few get to experience the kind that I imagine for myself. You always expect the fairytale, I don't care who you are, or who you're trying to kid, we all just want to be loved. It is predetermined human nature to desire something so simple but complex.

I came across something of a fairytale once or twice and got attached to the idea that they could be my happiness. But I was naïve to the fact that heartache exists in real fairytales and love stories. As you may have noticed, love is something that clouds my mind a lot as I get older and experience the world for myself. And yet it pains me to be in search of something so impermanent, yet fundamentally important to some.

It's a burden not to be loved.

But equally a burden to love another and not have those feelings reciprocated. You see, for an 18-year-old you might find it hilarious when I say I've always been an afterthought in terms of the people I've been with. But it's true, with Thor I was his escape from his crumbling relationship until he didn't need one anymore and with Home and Away Bae, he ended up choosing someone else in the end. I'm not sure how anyone can believe in love if that is how they are treated. The people who show you so much affection and hope of a future one minute and then leave you when you're done benefiting them the next don't exactly cut it for the ideal vision of love that I had imagined. So, I propose to you, a question. How can I waltz around with all the self-worth I think I am capable of, and expect someone to love me the way I wish for, for the full me, my mind, body and soul…if I cannot love myself due to the actions and mistakes of others?

This leads me on to the other relationships that we have explored to do with love. Let's start with mother dearest, the hardest yet easiest one. It's hard to remember a time when I felt love from her, and I didn't question it or cringe at its forced existence. I don't think she knew how to do the right thing by us, and even now if she was given the chance, I still don't think she'd be able to comprehend the kind of uncontrollable, consistent and loving bond of a mother and child. Its rare for me to talk about my future in this book, but that's because at times I didn't know if I'd have one, or how any positivity or happiness could come from such a miserable soul and story. I think because of her, and how I view her, the thought of a future with children in it is very daunting to me. The responsibility and preciousness of a child in my hands is far from imaginable for me. What if I became nothing but a mirror image of her, how could I love this child in the right way if I lacked a maternal bond with my own mother. And picture this, a child without grandparents? How could I deprive a baby of their human rights of a grandmother? And how would I explain all of this messed up, family nightmare to them innocent children?

I have dreams, just like any other person, but with dreams I have fears. And those fears are fueled by her actions that have brought us here and forced me to be the person I am. What if she has made me into someone that is so in need of a stable attachment that I am then unlovable? What if I am so insecure about trusting others and their intentions because of all these secrets and dark thoughts that no one sees me as worthy of staying with? Would I be stuck under a spell by just a "somebody" like she was? Or would I overcome these fears and be better than her?

Surprisingly after all these sad stories I have spilt to you, I have managed to get into university to study Law. This is something that seemed so far away for so long, and even I am shocked at myself for managing it. I am the first of us six children to get into university. I think this goes to show that every bad day eventually ends, and that no matter where you are or what's happening, you have the strength to move past it, because, hey, I did it. I want to learn, and protect those who need me, and with this course, I can make that possible. So, while I am questioning love, I guess it needs to be acknowledged that lack of it, doesn't necessarily mean all bad things, because I did this.

I think for someone like me, that has questioned love her whole life and its validity, that its only right to end this book with a question of love for you all. What would you have done in my mother's shoes? What does love mean to you? And, most importantly, I want you to think about your priorities in love. Yes, I think it's important to love, but if love turns harmful and wicked like it did to my family, promise me that you will give it up, promise me that these words have helped you understand that sometimes you are the only person that you need to love. Sometimes, regardless of everything, *you* have got to be the most important person. And whether that means just you, or the people you have created, nothing should come before that.

Love may conquer all, but not me.

Printed in Great Britain
by Amazon

35810913R00059